Ribbon Embroidery
With 178 Iron-On Transfers

J. Marsha Michler

DOVER PUBLICATIONS, INC.
Mineola, New York

For their contributions to this book, many thanks to:
Green Mountain Hand-Dyed Linens, P.O. Box 206, North Clarendon, VT 05759, for supplying naturally-dyed linen fabrics, excellent backgrounds for ribbon embroidery.
Things Japanese, 9805 NE 116th, Suite 7160, Kirkland, WA 98034, for "Dyeing in a Teacup" kit and supplies for dyeing silk ribbons.

Copyright

Bibliographical Note

Ribbon Embroidery: With 178 Iron-On Transfers is a new work, first published by Dover Publications, Inc., in 1997.

International Standard Book Number: 0-486-29818-3

Manufactured in the United States of America
Dover Publications, Inc., 31 East 2nd Street, Mineola, N.Y. 11501

Introduction

Embroidery stitches done in silk ribbon have a lovely dimensional quality, making embroidered flowers and leaves seem almost real. While most other types of embroidery bond with the background fabric, silk ribbon seems to float above it. Much of its appeal lies in this ethereal quality, and in how quickly and easily it works up. In its many possible applications, it is also extremely versatile.

Silk ribbon embroidery is often used to decorate personal accessories. Hats and hat-bands, belts, ties, scarves, hair ornaments, and slippers are some of the many items that can be made much more than ordinary with just a few stitches. Even the smallest motifs can be charming additions to articles of clothing, towels, and household linens. It can be used for beautiful accents on the tops of porcelain jars and wooden boxes, for mirror inserts, or fabric picture frames. Embellishment of quilts, cross-stitch, and needlepoint designs are a few more of its many creative applications.

Because ribbon provides greater coverage than thread, ribbon embroidery can be accomplished quickly. A small motif takes only a few minutes, with larger ones taking an evening or two.

Fabrics and Ribbons

Many types of fabrics can be used. Velveteen, velvet, linen, cotton, wool, and medium to heavy-weight silk make excellent backgrounds. Evenweave and plain-weave linens are easy to embroider, making them especially good for beginners. Sweaters, sweatshirts, jeans (especially ones that have been washed many times), socks, and T-shirts all are potential candidates for ribbon embroidery. Light-weight knits (such as T-shirts) and woven fabrics sometimes benefit from having a woven interfacing fused to their reverse side to provide a firmer base for the embroidery.

It is important to use quality ribbons. Filament silk ribbons imported from Japan are tightly woven and hold up well with minimal fraying and other problems. Also from Japan are 4mm-wide ribbons made of a synthetic protein fiber sometimes called "azlon." These feel and handle very similar to silk, are an excellent substitute, and are colorfast and washable.

The transfers in this book were designed for 4mm-wide (about 1/8″) ribbons, the most common width of embroidery ribbons. Silk ribbons also come in 2mm and 7mm widths. The 7mm ribbons, about 1/4″ wide, make wonderful woven roses and other flowers and leaves that will fill out a design quickly.

There are also 13mm, 18mm, and 32mm silk ribbons with finished woven edges, and several widths of bias-cut silk ribbons that have raw (unfinished) edges. Other ribbons made of rayon, cotton, polyester, nylon, and other fibers are heavier, and often stiffer than silk. The wider and heavier ribbons can be difficult to sew through fabric. Instead, use them to make gathered, ruched, or folded flowers and leaves, which are then sewn to the background fabric. They can also be couched for bows and streamers.

Hand-dyed silk ribbons are available in luscious shadings and colorations from subtle to outrageous. It is easy to dye them yourself using instant set silk dyes. There are many techniques for dyeing, including dip, speckle, marble, dye-painting, and others.

Silk and cotton threads, such as stranded flosses, and twisted "perles" or "buttonhole silks" can be used in addition to the ribbons. Use them to embroider fine stems and flower details. Beads, buttons, and charms can also be added to some motifs for a little extra pizzazz.

For ribbon embroidery supplies, please contact your local retailer or write: The Magic Needle, RR2, Box 172, Limerick ME 04048, enclosing $2.00 for a catalog.

Tools and Equipment

A size 18 chenille needle is recommended for 4mm and 7mm ribbons. This size needle will make a large enough hole in the fabric for the ribbon to slide through easily. If embroidery threads are used, a set of crewel/embroidery needles in assorted sizes will accommodate most threads. A sharp embroidery scissors is a must. A 4″ embroidery hoop is ideal for small motifs, a slightly larger one for larger designs. You should be able to reach the stitches easily.

Directions for Using Iron-on Transfers

Transferring the designs to your fabric is a fairly simple procedure. Here are directions for using these transfer patterns.

If the fabric is washable, preshrink and remove the sizing by laundering first. Iron carefully to remove all wrinkles. If the fabric ravels badly, it is a good idea to whip the edges by hand with an overcast stitch or to run a large zigzag machine stitch along the edges. Since transfers are made with very high temperatures which might melt synthetic fabrics, use a natural fabric such as cotton or linen. If you are unsure of the fibers in your fabric, test the ironability of the fabric first. For fabrics that will not withstand high temperatures, follow the directions for using iron-on transfers on dark fabrics, towels, and clothing

To prevent the motif from transferring to your ironing board, place an old sheet or other smooth fabric over the ironing board cover. To obtain a stronger impression of the pattern, especially after the transfer has been used, or on darker fabric, place aluminum foil on your board before pressing.

Before beginning any project, it is a good idea to test your iron, the fabric, and the evenness of your hand pressure. Cut out one of the little designs marked "Test Pattern" and follow the directions below for making a transfer. If the ink transferred well, you can proceed; if not, adjust either the heat or the length of time.

Use a dry iron set at medium or wool. Place the fabric on the ironing board, right side up. Cut out the desired motif, allowing a margin around the edges of the design. Pin the design to the fabric with the printed side down. Place the pins through the margins to hold the transfer in place on the fabric. Protect the iron by placing a sheet of tissue paper between the transfer and the iron.

Place the heated iron on the transfer and hold down for about 5 seconds. Apply a firm, downward, even pressure to all parts of the design, being specially careful to get the outer edges. Do not move the iron back and forth across the fabric as this will cause the transfer pattern to blur. After the transfer has been used once, add 2–3 seconds to the pressing time for each additional transfer.

Carefully remove one pin and lift one side of the transfer paper to see whether the complete design is indicated on the fabric. If not, replace the pin and repeat the process, concentrating on the area that did not transfer. Do not remove all the pins until you are sure the design has been successfully transferred. Once the pattern has been unpinned, it is almost impossible to register it to the fabric again.

When you are satisfied that the transferring has been completed, unpin the transfer paper and peel it off. You will want to save the transfer paper to use for additional repeats or to use as a check on the design. If the design is not clear enough, you can refer to the transfer sheet and reinforce vague areas on the fabric with a waterproof felt pen or laundry marker. Make sure that the ink is completely waterproof because just the moisture from the steam iron can cause the ink to run.

Using Iron-on Transfers on Dark Fabrics, Towels, and Clothing

Dark fabrics such as burgundy, hunter green, deep blue, and black, and velveteen and terry cloth, with their napped surfaces, make beautiful surfaces for ribbon embroidery; however, iron-on transfers are not a suitable method of transferring a design onto them. Also, on some pieces of clothing, you may not want to permanently mark the fabric. In these cases, one of the following two methods may be used to transfer a design.

Tear-away Transfer Method. Iron the design onto tear-away material and baste this to the front of the piece to be embroidered. Work the embroidery, then carefully remove the tear-away, trimming it with scissors if necessary. Avoid pulling the stitches out of place.

Tracing Paper Transfer Method. Trace the design onto tracing paper and lay this face down on the fabric (reversing the design as it would be if ironed on). Poke holes through the tracing paper, and, with a chalk pencil, make dots and light lines to mark the stitch placements. Refer to transfer pattern for the appropriate stitches to embroider.

To Embroider Clothing and Towels

Ribbon embroidery may be worked on collars, cuffs, pockets, around necklines, on shoulders, and on other parts of clothing. Use either transfer method above if permanent markings are not wanted on the clothing.

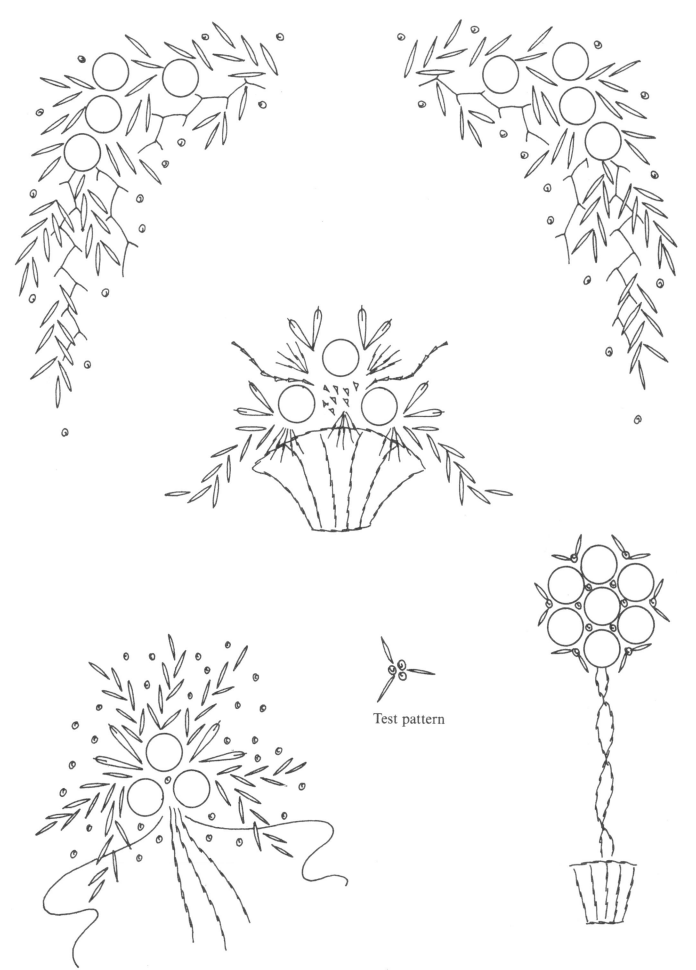

Test pattern

Plate 1

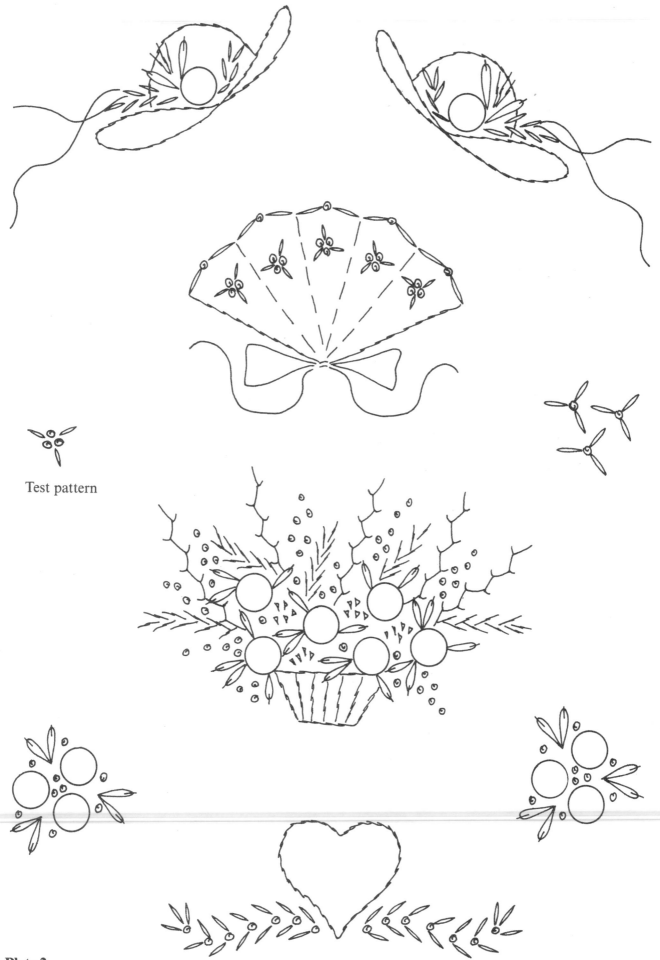

Test pattern

Plate 2

Test pattern

Plate 3

Test pattern

Plate 4

Test pattern

Plate 5

Test pattern

Plate 6

Test pattern

Plate 7

Plate 8   Test pattern

Test pattern

Plate 9

Test pattern

Plate 10

Test pattern

Plate 11

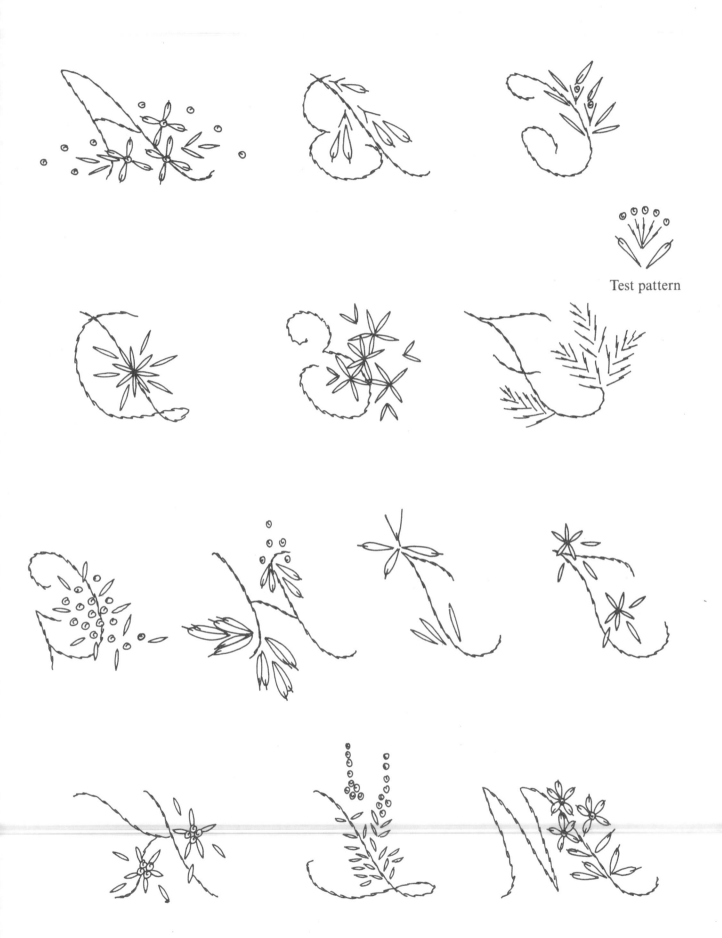

Test pattern

Plate 12

Test pattern

Plate 13

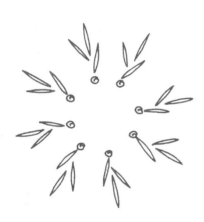

Test pattern

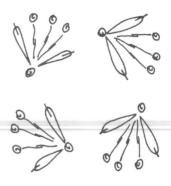

Plate 14

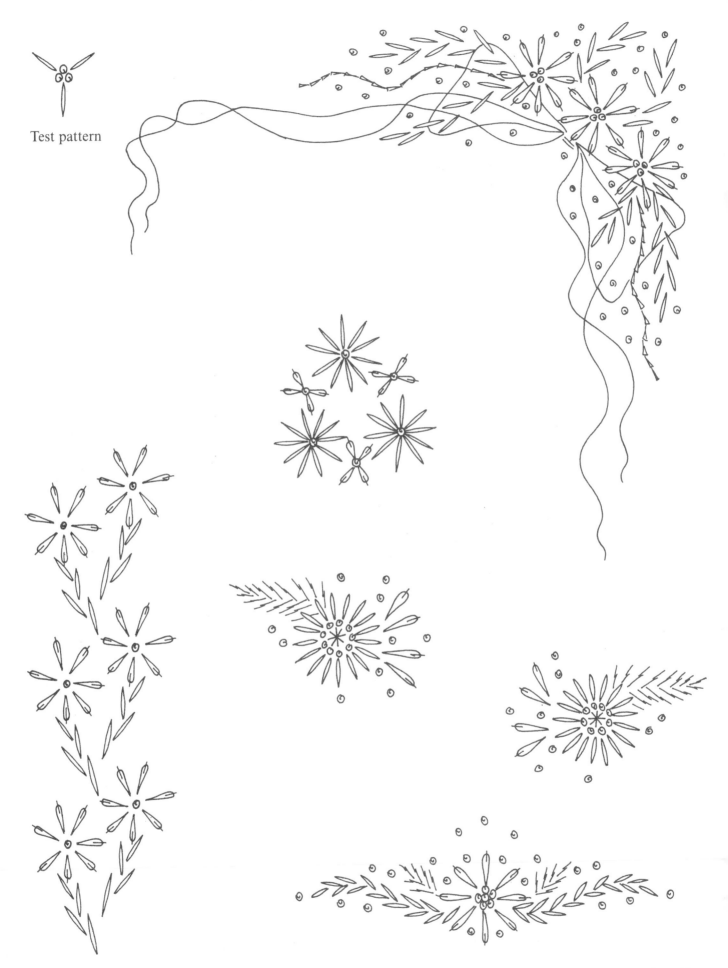

Test pattern

Plate 15

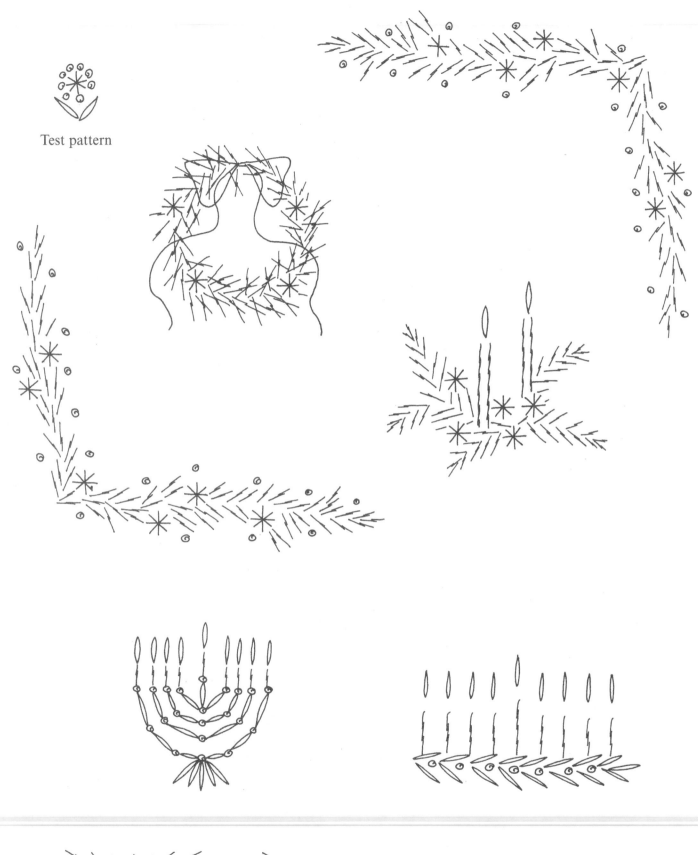

Test pattern

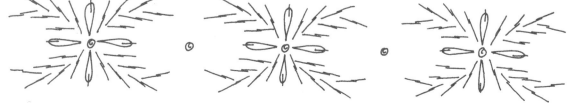

Plate 16

Test pattern

Plate 17

Test pattern

Plate 18

Test pattern

Plate 19

Test pattern

Plate 20

Test pattern

Plate 21

Test pattern

Plate 22

Test pattern

Plate 23

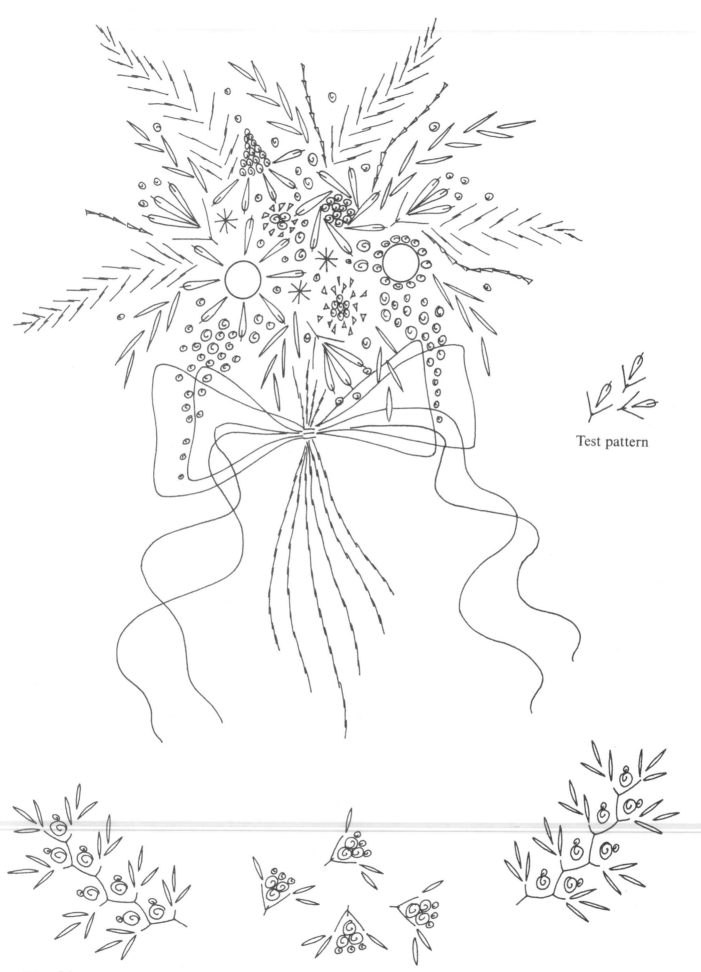

Test pattern

Plate 24

To embroider a T-shirt, first iron lightweight fusible interfacing onto the reverse of the fabric behind the transferred design. Cut it only as large as the outer edges of the design to avoid having the outline of the interfacing show through the fabric.

Ribbon embroidery is very effective on terry cloth towels, although it does require a little extra effort. Use the tracing paper transfer method to transfer a design. Embroider carefully, working the needle between the tufts of the terry cloth on both front and back sides of the towel.

Be sure the ribbons used on washable clothing and towels are colorfast. Washable synthetic ribbons are recommended for this purpose, but, if in doubt, prewash the ribbons and don't use them if dyes run.

Tips for Successful Ribbon Embroidery

1. Use a large needle. A size 18 chenille needle is recommended for 4mm and 7mm ribbons.
2. Use high quality ribbons intended for ribbon embroidery.
3. Use lengths of ribbon no longer than 12″ to 14″ to avoid fraying.
4. Allow the ribbon to untwist between each stitch. For ribbon, straight, and pierced loop stitches, hold the ribbon smooth with your thumb while making the stitch.
5. Ironing the ribbons before using them makes them extra smooth.
6. Make stitches locsely for natural looking flowers.
7. Be non-judgmental. Two stitches made identically will rarely look alike, a characteristic of ribbon embroidery that imparts individuality to your work.

If you are unfamiliar with the stitches, practice them on scrap fabric.

How to Begin

To fasten the ribbon onto the needle, a special locking technique is used. This allows most of a length of ribbon to be used, resulting in less waste. Insert about 2″ of the ribbon through the eye of the needle. Pierce this end of the ribbon with the needle, then pull on the longer end. A "knot" will settle onto the eye of the needle.

Fasten the ribbon to the reverse side of the fabric with a tiny stitch, placing it where it will later be concealed by embroidery. Bring the needle through to the front of the fabric, running it through the tail of this stitch. This locks the ribbon to the fabric without a bulky knot. To end a ribbon, make two or three tiny stitches on the reverse of the fabric, working these under previously made stitches to prevent them showing on the front.

Stitches for Ribbon Embroidery

Stitch Key

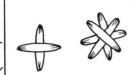

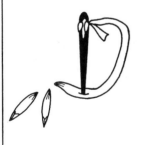
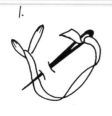

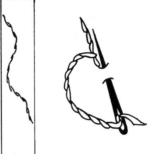

Straight Stitch
Remove any twists, then, holding the ribbon smooth with your thumb, pull through to the back.

Double Cross Stitch
Make four crossed straight stitches keeping the ribbon smooth.

Sheaf Stitch
Make three vertical straight stitches loosely, then "tie" them with a small stitch.

Twisted Straight Stitch
Roll the needle between your fingers to twist the ribbon before pulling it through to the back.

Ribbon Stitch
Hold the ribbon smoothly on the surface of the fabric. Pierce the ribbon at the far end of the stitch, and pull through slowly, stopping when the stitch has formed.

The stitch can be varied by making it slightly "poufed" instead of flat on the surface of the fabric.

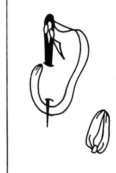

Twisted Stem Stitch
Work along the transferred line, having the ribbon twisted and the needle facing the previously-made stitch. Always keep the ribbon on the same side of the needle. Make stitches shorter to accommodate curves.

Fly Stitch
Form the stitch keeping the ribbon under the tip of the needle, pull through, then tack in place with a small stitch.

Long Stem Fly Stitch
The tacking stitch is longer and is sometime twisted.

Lazy Daisy Stitch
This is similar to the Fly Stitch. Make the stitch with the ribbon under the tip of the needle, pull through, and tack with a small stitch.

Long Stem Lazy Daisy
The tacking stitch is longer and is sometimes twisted.

1.
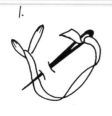
2.

Feather Stitch
Working downwards and keeping the ribbon under the tip of the needle, take stitches at opposite sides of an imaginary line.

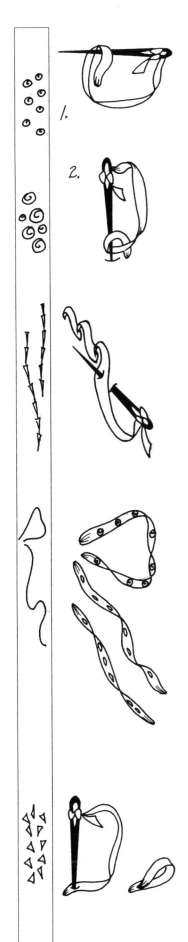

French Knot

For a small French knot, come up through the fabric, wrap the ribbon snugly around the needle once and pull through a short distance away.

For a larger French knot, wrap the ribbon loosely around the needle two or three times before pulling through. (The looser the wraps, the larger the stitch).

Plume Stitch

Work towards the previous stitch from the top downwards. Form a small loop of ribbon, hold it in place, and take a short stitch, going through the background fabric and then the ribbon.

Couching

Two separate ribbons are used. Fasten the first ribbon to the fabric and pull it through to the front. Then fasten a second ribbon and use this to make small straight stitches or French knots to hold the first ribbon in place along the transferred line. To finish, bring each ribbon to the back and fasten off.

Pierced Loop Stitch

Pierce ribbon with needle and pull it partway through to form a loop. Hold the loop in place while making the following stitch.

Loops can be 1/4″ or more in length.

ROSES

Stem Stitch Rose

Work stem stitch in a circular fashion from the center outwards. This rose can be started with one shade of ribbon and finished with another.

Woven Rose

Make five spokes using floss or embroidery thread, then, with ribbon, weave around and around to fill in. Wider ribbon makes a fuller rose.

Rose with French Knot Center

Make a cluster of five or six French knots, then work stem stitch around this center.

Stitch Variations

These can be added to the motifs as desired.

Work French knots on top of straight or ribbon stitchs.

Work a second ribbon stitch on top of a previous one. Use two shades of green to make two-tone leaves.

Lazy daisy and fly stitches can be tacked with French knots.

Make one lazy daisy stitch inside another. Two shades of ribbon may be used.

7

Stitching Suggestions

Most stitching can be done in any order. Where stitches overlap, work the background details first. Most of the couched streamers and bows are embroidered first, with later stitches overlapping them. Baskets are also worked before their contents. Stitches can be worked on top of previous stitches, although this must be done with care to avoid pulling them out of place.

For a fuller look, additional stitches may be added to motifs. French knots and ribbon stitch leaves make good fillers. Outlined designs can be filled in with the stitches of your choice; for instance, filling in hearts with French knots will give them a romantic look.

Make stitches slightly larger than the transfer to be sure to completely cover the lines.

The following are suggestions for some of the flowers and foliage shown in the transfer designs.

Blueberries: Work double cross stitch in blue, French knots in lilac, and ribbon stitch leaves in green.

Fuchsia flower: Make large, loose French knots, pierced loop, lazy daisy, and twisted stem stitches in shades of fuchsia and purple, or pink and cream.

Fern: Twisted straight stitches in shades of green.

Approximate Yardages

Actual yardage is dependent on the sizes of the stitches, the distance between them, and whether any ribbon is wasted, but the following will give you some idea of how much ribbon to purchase.

One yard of ribbon will make approximately:
9 woven roses or double cross stitches
30-36 ribbon or twisted straight stitches
12 lazy daisy or fly stitches

Care of Ribbon Embroideries

For washable pieces, wash by hand in cool water, rinse well, and line dry. Wrap the piece in a towel to absorb excess water before drying. To iron, place the piece on a terry cloth towel and press up to and around the embroidery. Do not press the embroidery itself.

Alphabet Flowers

The alphabet on Plates 12 and 13 has a flower or plant for each letter of the alphabet. These are:

Anemone	Narcissus
Bluebell	Orchid
Calla Lily	Peony
Dahlia	Queen Anne's Lace
Edelweiss	Rose
Fern	Sunflower
Gypsophila	Thyme
Hosta	Uvularia (Merrybells)
Iris	Veronica
Jasmine	Wisteria
Kalmia (Laurel)	Xeranthemum (Straw flower)
Lavender	Yucca
Mallow	Zinnia